THE BUG BOOK

by Sue Fliess

Grosset & Dunlap
An Imprint of Penguin Random House

To Dad, for teaching me to love even the tiniest of creatures—SF

GROSSET & DUNLAP
Penguin Young Readers Group
An Imprint of Penguin Random House LLC

Photo credits: front cover, page 1: (dragonfly) © Thinkstock/hawk111, (bee) © Thinkstock/Savushkin, (beetle) © Thinkstock/suksaeng, (caterpillar) © Thinkstock/InesWiehle, (stick bug) © Thinkstock/dreamnikon, (ladybug) © Thinkstock/GuidoVrola; back cover: (beetles) © Thinkstock/alice-photo, (grasshopper) © Thinkstock/GlobalP; page 3: © Getty Images/Stephen Simpson; page 4: (house fly) © Thinkstock/Ale-ks, (beetle) © Thinkstock/suksaeng; page 5: © Thinkstock/Savushkin; page 6: © Thinkstock/suksaeng; page 7: © Thinkstock/LiliKo; page 8: © Thinkstock/lnzyx; page 9: © Thinkstock/Daniel Nel; page 10: (pill bug) © Thinkstock/Alexey Romanov, (butterfly) © Thinkstock/boule13; page 11: (butterfly) © Thinkstock/boule13, (beetle) © Thinkstock/Tung-Tong; page 12: (crickets) © Thinkstock/lnzyx, (grasshopper) © Thinkstock/GlobalP; page 13: (foot) © Thinkstock/LucasSG83, (termite) © Thinkstock/DenBoma; pages 14–15: © 13/Chris Stein/Ocean/Corbis; page 16: © Getty Images/AFP; page 17: © Thinkstock/thomasmales; page 18: (bee) © Getty Images/Vitalii Hulai, (beetle) © Thinkstock/happymannt; page 19: © Thinkstock/User10095428_393; page 20: © Thinkstock/Henrik_L; page 21: © Herbert Kehrer/Corbis; page 22: © Thinkstock/KarSol; page 23: © Thinkstock/johnandersonphoto; page 24: (lice) © Getty Images/Sean Gallup, (middle and right bedbug) © Thinkstock/Smith Chetanachan, (left bedbug) © Thinkstock/smuay; page 25: (damselfly) © Thinkstock/Eric Isselée, (cockroach) © Thinkstock/mrkob, (ladybug) © Getty Images/Serghei Velusceac; page 26: © Solent News/Splash News/Corbis; page 27: © Thomas Marent/Minden Pictures/Corbis; page 28: (crickets) © Thinkstock/lnzyx, (praying mantis) © Getty Images/bozhdb; page 29: (firefly background) © hsimages/Westen61/Corbis, (firefly foreground) © Mitsuhiko Imamori/Minden Pictures/Corbis; pages 30–31: © Thinkstock/demidov; page 32: (bee) © Thinkstock/Savushkin, (metallic beetle) © Thinkstock/Tung-Tong, (cricket) © Thinkstock/lnzyx, (hawk moth) © Thinkstock/LiliKo, (rhino beetle) © Thinkstock/happymannt.

Library of Congress Cataloging-in-Publication Data is available.

ISBN 978-0-448-48935-3   10 9 8 7

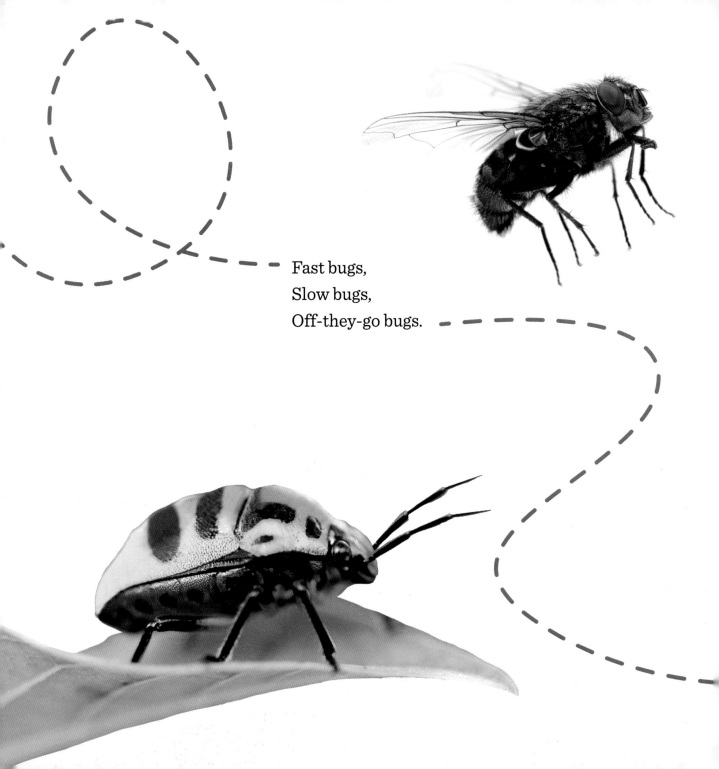

Fast bugs,
Slow bugs,
Off-they-go bugs.

Hop bugs,
Fly bugs,
Way-up-high bugs.

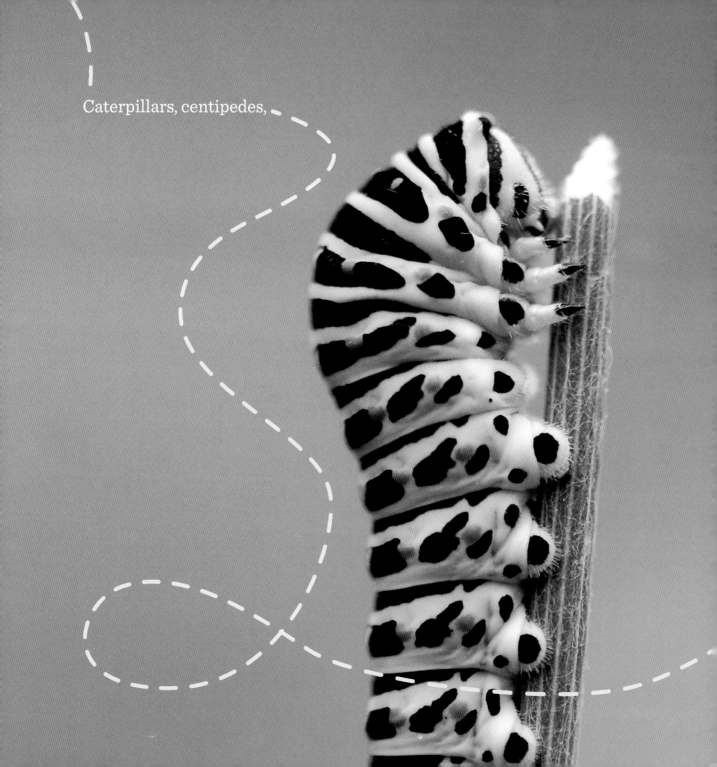

Caterpillars, centipedes,

Moths that fly at record speeds!

Creep bugs,
Climb bugs,
Sticky-slime bugs.

Turn bugs,
Squirm bugs,
Earthy-worm bugs.

Roly-polies, butterflies,
Bumpy bugs with bulging eyes!

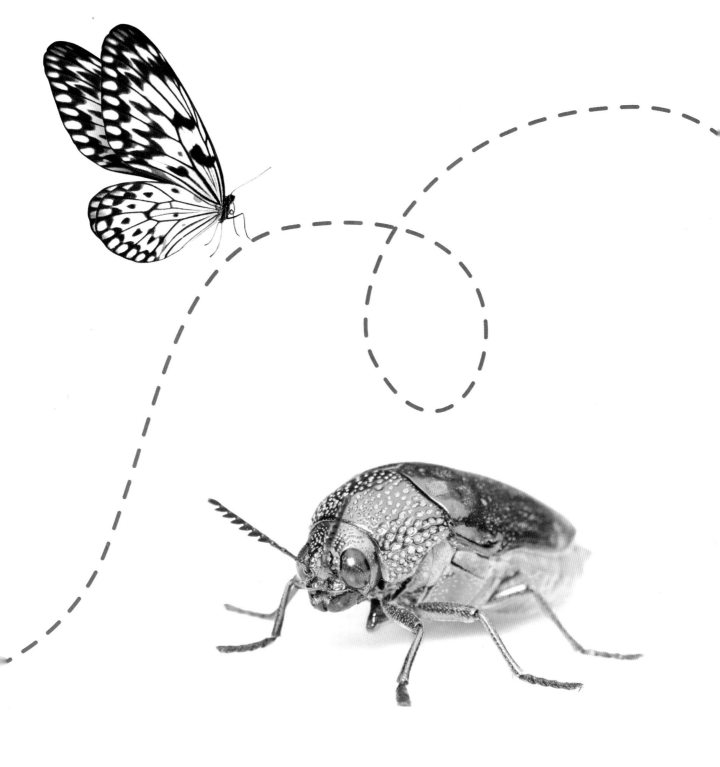

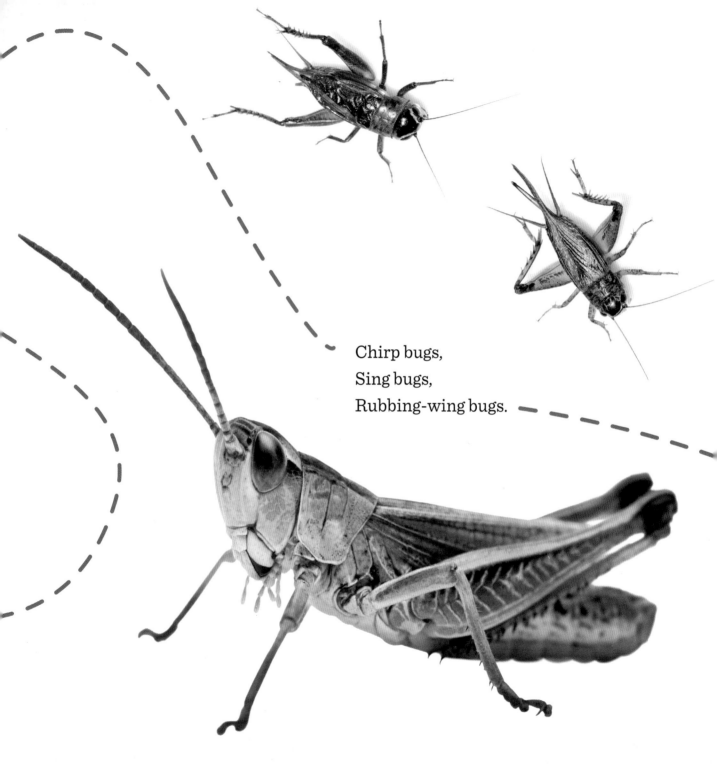

Chirp bugs,
Sing bugs,
Rubbing-wing bugs.

Shoo bugs,
Swish bugs,
Just don't squish bugs!

To the house and up the wall,
Ants go marching down the hall!

Sky bugs,
Land bugs,
Dig-in-sand bugs.

Swim bugs,
Glide bugs,
Water-stride bugs.

Beetles, spiders, bumblebees,

On the sidewalks,
in the trees.

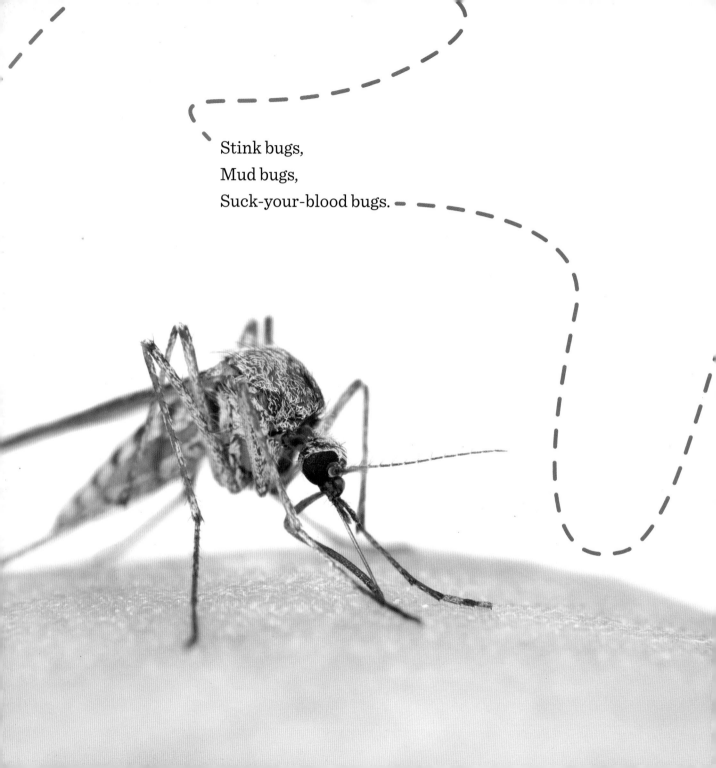

Stink bugs,
Mud bugs,
Suck-your-blood bugs.

Web bugs,
Spin bugs,
Got-stuck-in bugs!

Bugs that camouflage and bend,
Bugs with legs that never end.

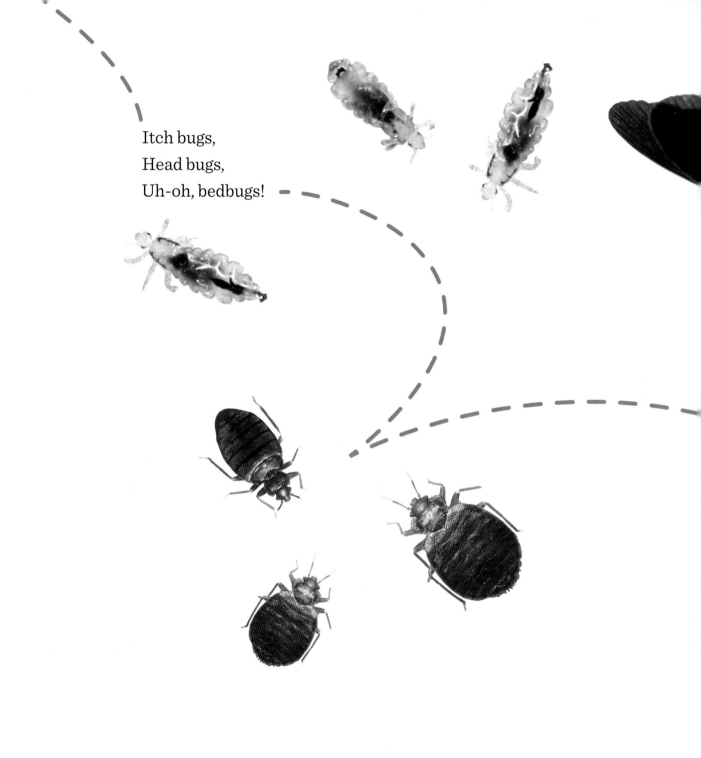

Itch bugs,
Head bugs,
Uh-oh, bedbugs!

Shy bugs,
Bold bugs,
Catch-and-hold bugs.

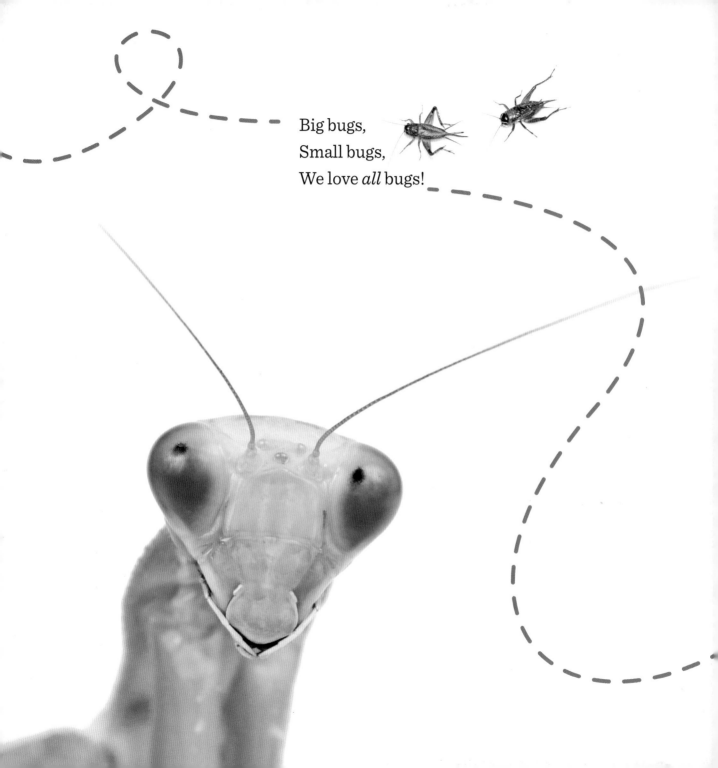

Big bugs,
Small bugs,
We love *all* bugs!

Day bugs,
Night bugs,
Tails-that-light bugs.

Bugs in beds of soil deep,
Dreamy bugs fall fast asleep.

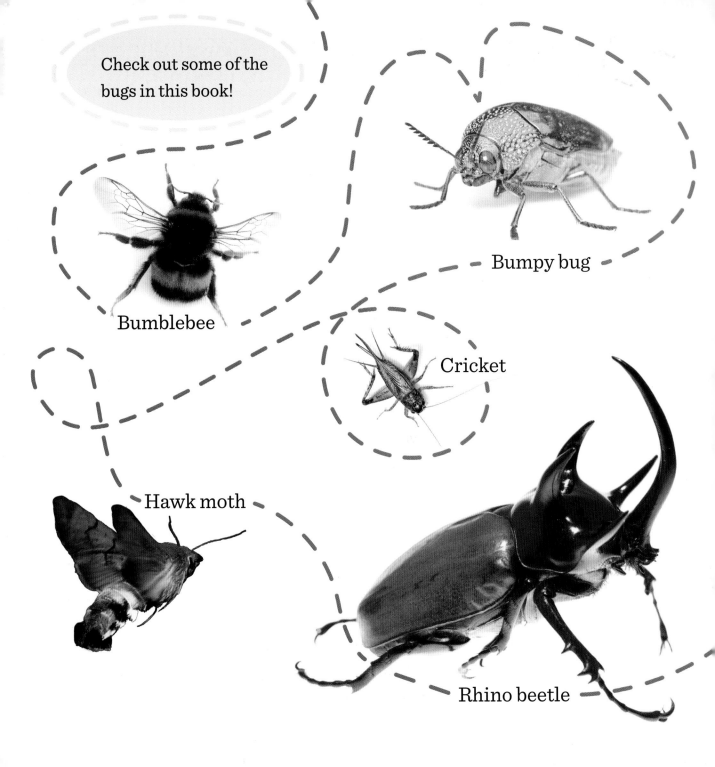

Check out some of the bugs in this book!

Bumpy bug

Bumblebee

Cricket

Hawk moth

Rhino beetle